He Wore Long Sleeves

Bilaal Muhammad

Contents

Alisha,
You have come into my life and made feel on top of the world. I thank you for all you have done for me. You make me smile. I love everything about you. From the follicles of your hair to the toes of your feet, you are beauty.

Love always

10/15/2014

"In memory of In Flora Ruby Johnson"

CHAPTER
ONE

Poet

Birthed by the sunlight!
Everyday life is the motivation
that guides the pen of the poet
and as he scribes words formulating

sentences that are designed to pierce
the souls of those that are torn to listen
to the lyrical libations.

He clicks his pen!

And with each click, click of his pen
he conjures up the souls of his ancestors
and he stands before the audience
and he strips himself bare.

Palms sweaty as he grips the mic,
but like the bass master who casts his line
in the ocean, hoping for the catch
of his life he waits patiently.

Trembling, trembling in fear.
Because a pool of eyes are watching
like the predator watches its prey
because somewhere in the audience

there's someone that really needs to hears
what he has to say. So, with arms out
stretched he spews out word after word,
line after line and sentence after sentence

he awakens those that hung
from oak trees for their rebellion.
And the night that Moses parted the red sea
there was a poet spitting poems that kept

the spirit of the weak and weary alive.
The Southern Geechee was ridiculed
by those not knowing that they were our link
to our African heritage.

Carrying the energy of the sun in my DNA
you cannot abort me for I am that I am.

Birth by the sunlight!

Terrorist attacks in Iraq intensified
once we set foot on their soil,
4000 plus Americans, annihilated because of our
leader's intent to monopolize on their oil.

But back home, for five days you ignored
the cries of the hurricane victims
in new Orleans, levees discovered to have
been destroyed by hateful and deceitful means.

So, rather I'm wearing a Brooks Brother's suit
or baggie jeans you, look at me with the same
discriminating grin, that reads,
I must remain noncompetitive with you

except in the area of sports and entertainment.
And we accept this, just watch how many
boys and girls being groomed to be our

next athletic or movie star icon.

But in the boardrooms of fortune 500 companies
it is your presence and mine that is non-existent.
So, the poet loses himself between the lines
of each page constructing his next love poem

but not your traditional man loving woman poem.
Relentlessly he writes, writes until
ink begins to flow through his pores
and the tips of his fingers are sore.

Faithfully believing that he'll soon reach
the soul that's desperately waiting
for resurrection.

Savannah

African drums were playing
in the background as I sat down
to record my thoughts. And as I
contemplated my next line I thought
of you.

And as my pen continued to manipulate
the page you appeared, twisting and
turning your body to each caress of
the djembe drum with the Savannah River

sliding by in the background.
(And yo, point of reference)

do not drink and try to
navigate on cobblestone
it's not a pretty sight.

A group of about thirty gather around
a saxophonist playing tunes from Motown
tracks of my tears and I shop around
takes me to a magical place.

Where the community was your extended
family, yeah we had our issues but parents
did not need cell phones or GPS systems
to get a fix on their children's location.

And as I maneuver through the thousand
or so visitors on River Street I feel at home
oblivious to the problems of the world

I could care less about what's going on.

And click, click, click is all I hear
from the would be photographers
documenting the moment
crowds halting traffic for hours.

My stomach growls with each inhale
of the delightful aromas
escaping into the air
from restaurants like One Eyed Lizzy.

And while at the intersection
of Abercorn and Bay Streets
I believe I saw my indigenous ancestors
performing an ancient ritual.

A machete in one hand and sugarcane
in the other and with one swipe of the
machete, I'm standing before a microphone
spitting poems while she dances to the

rhythm of my words. And with each dance
she tells how she cheated death

so I watch

and I watch

and I watch

until I see Venus in her eyes,
she's like magic music.

They say she's been around for years
hypnotizing millions with her seductive dance
so I ask.

Who are you?

She answers, they call me Savannah.

Haikus

Billion dollar bail outs and
war torn countries
are reminiscent of haikus,
you either get it or you don't.

So, help me to comprehend
why weeds are cut off at their roots
while asphalt fertilizes oak trees
and why do we say sunrise or sunset
when the sun doesn't move?

Perhaps if we pay attention to
the bee prior to being pricked
we will rise above the confusion
before going insane.

The harlot soars above a city saturated in sin
where senate seats are up for sell
like groceries at your local market.

Where future endeavors are met
with an ubiquitous death
so I learn to write love poems
until my thought patterns are restless.

And lyrical typhoons are written
in Sean Bell's blood
after 50 shots from the cops
so little black boys speak out.

Corporate CEO's travel to DC

with sign in hand that reads

will

work

for

government loan.

And life secrets are contained
within the concepts of mathematics
so take the pajamas off your mind
and wake up from your deep sleep.

Because literary libations are transferred
onto linen cloth
where honey coated teardrops
are bitter sweet.

So, who do we hold accountable?
For the many marches and the copious causes
where we shouted phrases like,
with no struggle comes no progress.
But when does the struggling stop?

It should be obvious that the entire
world is in a recession so stabilize
your position and move on.

Executive Bailouts

Yes we can reverberated throughout
the audience as he completed his speech
and now the sun shines brighter in Chicago
because its favorite son now resides at
1600 Pennsylvania Avenue.

Perhaps a brighter future lies ahead
but here's the thing, presidents are
part of a system that's been in place for centuries
and its modus operandi will remain intact
no matter who occupies the oval office.

And just maybe a few positive thinkers
will be inspired by this historical feat
but change only comes when change
from within is complete.

A woman sits alone pondering her next move
after she and her husband loses their careers.
The bailout of multibillion dollar companies
will not stop the foreclosures or this woman's tears.

So now murder suicide appears
to be their only way out
six innocent children murdered by the hands
of their parents.

How's that for a bailout?

Stimulus packages benefits the millionaire
while the minimum wage employee

succumbs to the great waves of bills crashing
ashore. Too ashamed to answer his phone
and afraid to answer his door.

And somewhere in America
a poet sits watching the inauguration
salivating over the possibilities of new poems
that will inspire the next generation.

Who knows?
Maybe the revolution has come.
Picture the celebrations held in cemeteries
Malcolm, Martin, and Marcus
may our ancestors now rest in peace.

Distracted by the articulate leader no one seems
to notice that the expectations are high as hell
two wars a crippling economy
and a health system that's primed to fail.

Confetti like words are thrown around
ricocheting off eardrums and coming back
full circle through the mouth of babes.

They speak of "hope, history and change."

But for now, unemployment reaches record
Numbers and homes are auctioned off
like a Van Gogh, millions are jobless,
hungry, and have nowhere to go.

State employees receives I owe you's
while money hording CEO's lavishes

in 18 billion dollar bonuses
and the average Joe
let's just say your stimulus check
will not carry that many zeros.

Mental Revolution

Like the mummified pharaohs that lay
in the Egyptian tombs I sometimes feel
trapped in this cocoon called America.

Where I am expected to work for
minimum wage and die penniless
and broke.

But like candy coated rain drops
I walk barefoot in the park so that I can feel
the earth's bio-rhythms beneath my feet.

And not worry about entertaining
the never ending question.

Yo! Where are your shoes?

I am viewed as anti-sociable because
I like to be left alone at the precise time
the sun walks across the Atlantic.

I stand erect like Orion with my bow
in my hands as I hunt for wisdom,
while this corrupt system search for
ways to keep me locked in their mental prisons.

They feed me from poisonous trees
that bears poisonous fruit with no
nutritional value.

So, I keep a keen eye on the alphabet

soup groups, who are infiltrating poetry venues
with their smart phones taking pictures and
notes on every revolutionary poet.

Emailing their findings to big brother
who's waiting for the one word, one phrase,
or one line that will facilitate in the
remapping of our minds.

Because the only way we will ever
emancipate ourselves from this vulture
like nation is through higher education.

You got secret societies claiming that they're
here to keep the secrets sacred.
But the only secret they're keeping sacred
is their conspiracy to perform together,
an illegal, wrongful, or subversive act against you.

The crisis in the Persian gulf as grave as it is,
also offers a rare opportunity to move toward
a historic period of cooperation.

That's what they want you to believe
but peep this. The quantity of food available
to the poorest groups' people will simply
be insufficient.

And that's when they're gonna implement
their human reproduction management.
They will prevent the unauthorized natural
conception by putting contraceptive chemicals

in the water supplies, or certain essential foods
you buy. And quiet as kept, that's already being
done. Money is and has been, the most important
and powerful tool in the capitalist's bag of tricks.

Freedom, privacy, and independence
is what their cash represents.
But government insiders want to do away
with it. By first changing the color of our

currency then having us exchange our old
money at the u.s. treasury.
And in return for of our paper money
we will receive new cards called Americards

each biomechanically impregnated
with the owner's hand and retina prints.
And that's just the start of it…

Scattered Thoughts

He writes while on the move using
whatever he can get his hands on.
Not wanting to stop to look for his
journal while he is on fire with ideas.

Stanzas one and two are written on
the back of a Whole Foods bag while
the title of his poem is scribbled
alongside the name Starbucks
as he enjoys his morning cup of java.

Conversations are often interrupted with
the stroke of a pen across his palm
eyes fixated like a sniper on target.

And with one shot from his pen another page
bleeds with envy. While at work he thinks
about how he can improve his latest creation
so the napkin that he uses to clear the obstruction

from the corner of his mouth is his newest victim.
(Readers of poetry have ringside seats to the psyche
of poets, he writes), then the napkin is jammed inside

his right front pocket for later examination.
His thoughts are somewhat scattered
but it all makes sense in the end, like when
he writes about how good his childhood was
when compared to the children of today.

We didn't have Xbox, PlayStation

or the internet, we, we played games like
hide and go seek, kickball, dodge ball, hopscotch,
and on occasion sat down with the girls and played
jacks.

And somewhere on his book shelf
there are more lines to his poem jammed between
pages 18 and 19 in the book The Art of War.
I don't know about you but I remember in my
creative writing class the teacher going on about

creating the perfect writing situation, like sitting
in a quiet cabin overlooking the lake and allowing
your thoughts to consume you.

Nah, he doesn't work like that because the moment
is fluid, fleeting and forever mutating so he writes
whenever the inspiration comes. And when it comes
he's a slave to it, he gotta put a pen to it so he writes.

And it doesn't matter if it's a complete stanza
or just one sentence he writes.

Ten Minutes

Ten minutes is all I need to write,
write and meditate on the hate
that have many souls waiting
at heaven's gate, sweating bullets
wondering if it's too late,

too late to do all they had to do,
when they had to do, what they had
to do. So I sit in my comfortable chair

and grab my pen and pad and bleed into
these pages, where I succumb to those
blue lines anticipating self-preservation
but those endeavors have been put on the

back shelf. Because life is centered
around false hopes and petty dreams
that pulverizes wonting teens, thoughts
of suicide takes residence in their brain,
tick   tock   tick.

A human time bomb detonation unknown
so now American skies are secured with drones
no more expectation of privacy not in
your persons, papers or homes.

This administration decided that assassination
of its own citizens is fair game, so you can best
believe that if you are considered a threat
this government will bring the pain.

So in ten minutes I write, write to clear my thoughts,
write for those standing at the cross roads
mind whirling like a tornado, life shredded
like dread locks caught in a battle between the
haves and have not's. So I kick off my sandals

and walk barefoot on the earth reaching out
to my ancestors,

give me

the strength

to carry

this load.

Gunshots and liquor shots, dawn of
the living dead, money wasted on
lottery tickets I'm sick, sick in my head.

Pen to pad, cut me,

pen to pad, cut me,

pen to pad cut me, and I'll bleed poetry.

Red and white blood cells
full of nouns, pronouns, verbs, and adjectives
backed by metaphors, similes, and hyperboles
give me a bic, parker or skilcraft that's
all I need.

To expose the true lies, lies. You say weapons
of mass destruction, I see nothing
but well-orchestrated corruption.

Congressional hearings on athletes
using performing enhancing drugs
but for some reason this system
is unwilling to prevent our self

destruction from the abuse of prescribed
and illicit drugs. So writing is my safe house
my pen is locked and loaded and my
target is in sight therefore I write
terminating every evil entity with
W
O
R
D
S
And yes I am blessed, blessed because
my human rights can never be taken
I was born free and like Malik El Shabazz
there is no whisper in me, amplified
by my heart mic not needed so I blog,
Facebook or tweet it.

So comment, share it, friend me,
or just tag alone
and you will see, that all I have to give
is my pen and some poems.

Twice Murdered

Here we are once again standing
at the threshold, murder of another
young black male, and the murderer
eludes jail. Found not guilty in a

court of their law. The prosecution failed
to prove beyond a reasonable doubt that
Zimmerman committed murder, the
evidence presented was weak therefore
not guilty is the verdict.

However the acquittal does not dismiss the
fact, that Zimmerman targeted Trayvon
because he was young, hooded and black,
so he lured him further into the dark, waiting

for the right moment to attack. It was a rainy
night in Sanford Florida, listening to his mp3
all he wanted to do was deliver a bag of skittles
and Arizona tea, but his journey was interrupted

by a misguided vigilante. Hunted down by a gun
carrying cop wannabe, 9-1-1 dispatcher, I have
a suspicious black male walking through the
neighborhood, and this guy looks like

he's up to no good. Stand down, do not pursue,
instruction ignored, so he pursued Trayvon
until he could run no more. 2013 and young
black males are still considered nothing but

prey, in 1955 Emmitt Till was murder in a similar
way. How long, how long must we endure such
racism, by the age of twenty five, I'm either
dead, jobless or serving life sentences in prison.

Exhaustion kicked in so he looked within,
there's no more room for flight, for his life
he must fight, 17-years-old at that very
moment he lived every black man's plight.

Fighting for his life moving through all
obstacles, but now he's face to face with
his enemy knowing he must now fight with
all his muscle.

So like a warrior he engages his adversary,
blow after blow he yells for help
but help is nowhere to be found, so he pounds
and pounds his captures' head into the ground.

Witnesses stood far off and did nothing to render
aide and 45 seconds later there he lay
never to see another day, never will his mother
hear him say, I love you and it will be okay.

But it's not, because in America the young
black male is despised because the world
knows he will someday rise like a pharaoh
thought pattern is not shallow

so he will lead nations not follow. But on
a rainy night his life was squeezed out
of him, along with parents millions will

mourn him. And George Zimmerman,

Your plan was premeditated in your car
full of rage you waited, it is said that
racial slurs were uttered, from Emmitt
Till, Sean Bell, and Trayvon Martin
a nation of young black males are
twice murdered.

Mommy's Secret Diary

When she was pregnant with
her child she vigorously prayed
for a girl, pretty smile and
little Debbie curls.

And when that fateful day arose
Glenda lying on her back with
legs in stirrups and painfully
curled toes.

The doctor delivered the news,
you have a healthy baby boy.

Now those tears running down her cheeks
were not the tears of joy
because Glenda did not want to raise
the illegitimate child of her rapist.

Reginald was the given name but
Regina was stuck in the back of
Glenda's brain.

So in her diary she secretly writes
as she tries feverishly to forget
that terrible night.

When her rapist tore into her over,
and over, and over again and into
her vagina he spilled his semen.

And at that moment she knew that she

conceived so she prayed while on
her knees.

Please give me a girl?

I regret the days when I would dress
my son up like a girl and call him
Regina. Then parade around the house
as sexy as I can and tell him
that this is how you attract men.
As Reggie read line after line he could
not believe the deceit that was mastered
mind by his mom.

The gravity of the revelation was too
heavy for him to bare, so he gave into
the voices from the drug dealers that
were buzzing in his ear.

He learned the drug game well so well
that he attracted the attention of DEA agents
and now he's severing a 10-year stretch without bail.

What he read in his mother's diary
severely plagued his mind. The
memories of wearing dresses made
it easy for Reggie to allow his cellmate
to penetrate him from behind.

And during her weekly visits Glenda's
eyes would swell. The sight of seeing
Reggie wearing a wig, high heals
and red lipstick rekindled Glenda's hell.

The day that she was raped she prayed
for a girl pretty smile with little
Debbie curls and her name is Regina.

The Corner

Street pharmacists prescribes illicit
Medication that keeps our future leaders
and teachers sedated, hooked on ideologies
that leaves them in a state of confusion.

While believing and depending on a system
that perpetuates the eternal strangulation
of young black males.

Ass out while serving hard time in jail,
ass out while being raped and abused in jail.

And on the corner is where the mis-education begins
amethyst rocks replaced by crack rocks
blinded by the paper chase that
keeps your mind locked.

Cellophane walls have you trapped
like the slave ships that transported you
through the middle passages through
then enslaved you through time.

Time, time, time waits for no one
but moves as one then returns to
the beginning of time
where we existed as echoes.

And where the Dogon tribe pinpointed
the exact location of Sirius a, b, and c
no telescopes needed just mental elevation.
But today's deaf, dumb and blind

are defecating on our ancestors legacy
with catchy hooks and spell bounding melodies.
Cash rules everything around me cream get
the money dollar, dollar bill ya'll.

And the hustle, the hustle appears to be
the only exodus out of the ghetto.
Sex, lies, and video tape big brother's on
the take squeezing you hard for a percentage
of every dollar you make.
So trying to accumulate those Benjamins
causes you to commit unspeakable sins
as you transcend from boys to men.

Where dead bodies has no ill affects
you step over them like stepping
over sidewalk cracks.

Symphonic gunshots produce everlasting sleep
while the daydreamers are victimized
by the predators that prowl the streets.

Hiding deep, deep in the shadows of the night
using their nocturnal powers trying to evade
the sirens and lights.

So we poets choose to be the vocal advocates
that will fight for their life right here, right now
on the corner.

Pen-Thoughts

When one speaks at the wrong time he often realizes that silence was the better of the two options.

Words are like bullets, once fired they cannot return.

The deaf hears not a sound but acknowledges the truth when heard. Open your ears and hear this truth.

Stay away from cluttered thoughts, for as you think you are.

A tear is pain freeing itself from a wounded or broken vessel.

Study every aspect of life and inherit completeness.

The ancestors say in seven breaths you must have the spirit to break through the other side.

The end is important to all things. So honor your beginning so that your end will ring true.

CHAPTER
TWO

The Letter

When was the last time
you wrote or received a love letter?
A love letter, not an email.

I'm talking about that old-fashioned,
pen on paper note that you actually
put into an envelope, stamp and
then send via the post office.

The art of writing like the dinosaur
has become extinct. We are in the era
of instant data sharing either by email
or texting your love on your PDA or cell phone.

I can remember the rush I felt sitting
before a piece of white lined paper with
pen in hand preparing to express my
undying love.

I mean my head would nod back and
forth like that heroin addict after injecting
his veins with that hot liquid love.

We are technology geeks giving in to
the convenience of a delete button
or spell check to disguise the imperfections.
What's next virtual sex?

Receiving a love letter sealed with a kiss or
her favorite perfume made me feel on
top of the world.

Now it's a pre-written text like, let's meet
or whacha doing? So impersonal
I don't know about you but I miss
those occasional paper cuts and ink stained

finger tips that are associated with writing.
So today, I'm gonna write a love letter,
a love letter to that special someone,
or maybe even to myself just for nostalgia sake.

Wind Song

Out stretched arms heart pounding
anticipation nipping at my heels
I shiver at your slightest touch.

While in your arms I go limp,
the dancing begins
with the wind beneath our feet
we begin to rise.

With you I have reached heights
never before achieved
mountaintops are our ballroom
and the ocean our dance floor.

As you gracefully take the lead we
bathe in the rays of the sun soaring
above the clouds no worries to think about.
We dance into the night to our song.

She Be Poetry

She approached the microphone
like a quiet storm captivating me
with verbal tornadoes mental
hurricanes and 100 mph syllables.

She greeted the audience while
adjusting the microphone then jumped
right into her poem.

As each word caressed her luscious lips
I watched in awe
I hung on her every Word.

It was astonishing how she made
me feel when she sat down to write
her poem. I was attracted to her.
Not because of her beauty but rather

for love and passion she has for her people.
At the climax of her poem the audience clapped
and cheered then a moment of silence.
As she looked out into the crowd
as if searching for someone.

Suddenly she began her next poem and like the first
I was sprung as I imagined her wearing a thong
she's the sweetest love poem.

She educated me on things I never knew took me
to places I never knew existed, not by
car train or plane she merely used her words.

Unable To Remember Yesterday

We shared the same passion the same
dreams. We were brothers not in the
biological sense but his mother was
my mom and my mom his mother.

They referred to us as the bopsey twins
we were inseparable.

But I went off to college and he, he
traveled to Parris Island, not for
vacation but for what would be his
eventual annihilation.

During his stay at Parris Island he
learned to be a killing machine armed
with grenades and a m16. He was sent
on a mission to snuff out another
man's dreams.

But what he learned on Parris Island
did not prepare him for what was waiting
on the battle field.

Where children would walk up to you
and offer you a shoe shine but in reality
was nothing but a walking suicide bomb.
How do you prepare for that?

Ultimately he had to assimilate the
mind of an assassin a ruthless
terminator and like a tornado leaving

dead bodies in its wake.

Just to survive such and ordeal but his
fate was sealed the night that he
and his band of brothers invaded this
village searching for the enemy.

To their surprise they walked right
into an ambush. Fifty men fighting for
their lives bombs, bullets, bullets, bombs.
When the fire fight stopped nineteen young men
were left standing dazed and confused amid
the rubble wondering.

What in the hell just happened here?

Thirty one men died for a senseless cause and
the loss of my brother has me in the land of oz.
I still remember hearing nothing but the
pounding of my heart when I received the
call mom told me your brother was killed in action.

Just hearing those words sent me back to
yesterday but for some reason I'm unable to
remember yesterday because yesterday.

Andre and I were sitting on the stoop at
the end of the day trying to count the stars
and with our mortal minds trying to reach
that far.

We would be the proud owners of B & A's
Jazz Club where he would play the saxophone

and I would recite poetry standing behind
the microphone but that dream is now gone.

I know I promised our mothers that
I would visit his grave site.
But how do I get them to understand?
That the cemetery is a place for the
physical dead and that my brother
Dre lives on in my heart and my head.

We communicate whenever there is a need.
Do I really have to follow the old tradition
of trying to find solace surrounded by a
bunch of granite and trees?

No, if you're looking for me I'll be sitting
on the stoop at the end of the day trying to
count the stars and talking to my brother Andre.

Metallic Beaches

Fiery red hair and eyes as cool as
the spring grass. She said that her
butter scotch colored complexion
comes from tanning on metallic beaches.

Because she is fed up with the incessant
sexual advances she receives from the
one eyed headed species, that lie next
to her in the sand.

So she retreats to her metallic beaches
where she reminisces on the days when
she was knee high to a grasshopper.
And when her beauty and sexuality

did not matter to whomever joined
her in the sand box.

Luv Deep

Sometimes,
sometimes I think we argue
just to speak and that just
frustrates me.

Because if you measure our relationship
from all the moans and groans that goes
on in between the sheets you would think
that we were in love deep.

But that's far from the truth.
It appears that you're only happy when I
rise your between your thighs or when you're
on top enjoying the ride.

And I'm not even sure if what we have is
right or wrong but I long for the
day when you share your inner
most fears as I share with you
mine and we laugh at each other's stale jokes.

I want to hear you say you love me
without having to kiss that hot spot
on the back of your neck or without
all the interruptions from each climax.

A verbal tango for two or a mental waltz
would do and in your ear I will sincerely
whisper that I love you.

Do you feel the same way I do?
Or are you cool with our physical
relationship?

Or is it that I'm reading too much into it
rambling on like someone suffering from
schizophrenia paranoid as shit?

But if you can relate just take my hand
and let's stroll down lover's lane
where I will name a star for you and for me
you'll do the same.

But if that's not cool with you then I'll
continue you to please you between the
sheets where I fantasy about being
in love deep.

Echoes of a Torn Soul

Trapped in a silicone sphere
she whispers in my ear
life is merely an illusion interwoven
into the perception of reality.

She smiles and I hear the melodies
of a bride gowned in white
prepared to take me on a journey
of many life times.

Her heart is the throne of life forms
unknown star systems and galaxies
are born through her majestic womb.

Perspicuous wisdom and sweet
like the honey dew many were
tested but were not worthy
to nibble on her dew.

Her breast touches my hands as
we stare into each other's eyes
where I see cotton candy skies.

The grains of the sand tells the
story of her infinity is her.
I try desperately not to see the
images of her but she has power

over me like the wind forces the
leaves to dance to her breeze.
I want to caress her buttery soft skin

and her spinal cord while I'm lost
within her mysterious place.

I'm not supposed to be here. Why
am I here?

Visions, thoughts, hopes and dreams
pure volcanic eruptions are what you'll
find trapped within a love sick man's dreams.
Then she left, left me standing here in
the chapel waiting to proclaim my vows
that I will forever love her.
Falling, deep, deep into the center of
the universe which changes into

a multi-verse that sends me to the
other side. Where I see unicorns with naked
women saddled riding in the fields
and ironically they all look like her.

I decide to donate my eyes to avoid
seeing the images of her but she
continues to haunt me.
So I reach into the cavity of my chest

and tear out my heart and with each
pulsating beat. My soul is torn, it echoes
I'm not supposed to want her but I just can't
live without her.

On The Move

As I awake from my sleep around
2 in the morning on my 40th birthday
she came to me.

And explained that she was on the move,
on the move for one last time
and I would never see her again.

Her words vibrated through me
like the roaring sound of thunder,
because they meant that she was
moving on, on to the next life.

Returning to the very essence that
sent her here with a purpose, to raise
four men whom she could be proud of.
And during the course of raising those

four men, times were hard, times were
extremely hard. Although she never
showed any sign of quit she experienced pain,
pain that a mother conceals from her children so,
they can incessantly enjoy their childhood.

We never could understand how she
could take what little food we had
and feed the entire neighborhood.

However, we were eye witnesses to the many
blessings she would receive for her
unselfish character.

Particularly one day she and my oldest brother
walked to the market with only twenty dollars
but when they returned, they walked through
the door with about two hundred dollars' worth
of food.

She was the strength and salvation for many,
wisdom dance to sweet melodies in her eyes.
She fought her entire life for the survival
of her children and when she was
presented with one last battle she
decided that it was time to go home.

Can I Love You

Can I love you until the sun sets
and the stars rise
until the smile from your lips touch the
essence within my eyes?

Can I love you until the reign becomes
a raging storm
or at least until an ocean begins to form
in the center of your core?

Yes, yes, you can love me until
the sun's horizon has bowed to
our supremacy, and the stars sing
our praise.

And as I witness the tears of joy dance
the dance of love down your cheeks
I will come to you with open arms.

Can I love you and become the goddess of
your dreams until you form echoes in my
soul of realities?

Can I love you until you rename me the
sun and the moon, until you stroke the
butterfly so it emerges from its cocoon or
we create our own melodies and
dance to our own tune?

I want you to love me, love me to the point
of multiplicity so, that in a thousand years

our love will still reign.

And we will ascend mountaintops where
the wind dances between us and the rays
of the sun bathes us as we walk
with the gods.

So share with me my heart, share
with me my eyes, share with my
my ears, so that you can hear, see
and feel as I.

Can I love you until I feel the wind beneath
my feet, until we merge become one and are
complete, until my will, mind and knees go weak
until I can't breathe, think or speak?

Can I love you? Love you like freshly fallen
snow, untouched by molested hands pure.
Can I love you? Love you so that you
do not see me as black, white,
Puerto Rican or Asian,
just simply your love.

Yes, yes you can love me for the pure…joy of
discovering what it is that makes us…we
and I too will open my arms, but at the
same time extend my mind to welcome you openly.

Yes, you can love me until I'm color blind
or not of sound mind… either way I'll only
see you because I have an angel's view
of what it is to be loved through and through

which can only be compared
to…..nothing.

Can I love you?

Yes, you can love me and I will love
you and we will be love.

Sagittarius

Tall beautiful and brown
intellectual conversations
birth mental orgasms ripe as the sun.

She loves me, me loves she
pure electric magnetic connection
In the mirror I see her reflection.

She's my goddess and I her god
strong, graceful and nurturing
mother of the universe.

My wounds healed by her touch
my pain eased by her words.
Upon her bosom I lay my head
as she feeds my hunger with her bread.

She has an angelic smile that will
take your breath away.
She'll take you into the night
and love your pain away.

Her liquid love is eternal
and I long to dine in her pleasures
so I too can see eternity.

Chances Are

A chance meeting that's all it was
beautiful brown eyes caught mine
suddenly I'm struck by the L bug.

She's about 5'10 (or maybe just an inch taller)
with ebony smooth skin.
And her smile reminded me of the exotic scents
cascading off the waves of the Nile
during ancient times.

Drop dead sexy is the adjective that
came to mind as she sat next to me
on the express train.

How you doing love?

She responds with a hesitant smile,
please don't be alarmed,
I just had to speak.

I turned away and continued to listen to my
mp3 and as my head swayed to the music
intimate scenes came to mind like,
me going for a ride in her little red corvette

while her fingers gently caress my shoulders
and back. Her embrace soft yet firm happiness
followed by sorrow envelops me at every turn.

A chance meeting that's all it was beautiful

brown eyes caught mine.

Will I ever see her again?

Love Struck

She has long black locks
and skin as smooth as chocolate
and pretty enough to make me
unlock the chamber of my heart.

So I approached with knot knees,
twisted tongue, and brain numb
but the words that shot fourth were
elegant enough to make her come.

Walk with me through the historical
part of the city of our birth
where I told her that we should be
together and if she let me be her man,

it could get no better. I want her to know
that she is like oxygen, essential
and I need her as much as I need to take
my next breath and know that great things
would be achieved after she and I get undressed.

Because I will massage away her pain and scars
and with a soft whisper
we will dance with the moon and stars.

This universe will give honor to our union
because I am not afraid to tell the world
that I am proud to come home to this woman.

And prepare a bath scented with scents of the Nile
a light kiss on her forehead is awarded

with an angelic smile
which keeps me satisfied for a while.

She is priceless, like the jewel that has not been
found yet and I am fortunate to have the
opportunity to get to be with a woman that
makes my eyes wet.

Yeah I know I sound whipped, but a strong
Woman will stand next to a man with soft words,
and wisdom like Solomon and when the
time is right she will let me slide inside
her essence.

Is it physical, no it's more than that
I feel her in my thoughts,
smell her in my dreams
where our love is manifested on sunbeams.

She is the food for my soul
the water that quenches my thirst
I want to be held by her
like the way she caresses her designer purse.

Days with her moves like molasses
where the concept of time has no place in this
evolution of our connection.
And you know what? In the mirror I see
her reflection.

I do not pretend, I ascend in the magic of
her love loneliness no longer exist
she is all that I need so my nine to five is

making sure that she is pleased.

I never thought that I would meet such
a woman on this journey called life
but I did, and that woman is my wife.

Pen-Thoughts

Contemplation is evidence of existence.

Praise and criticism are one and the same. They both massage your ego.

The blind man stumbles not, but he who has eyes hit all obstacles.

Behind every disaster there's a story to tell.

Walk in the light of the sun as if all can see you at all times.

A lonely child gazes out of his window looking for nothing in particular. He just wants a ray of hope.

The body is emptiness. Emptiness is form

Man can study many truths and still be in accord with his own truth.

Like the hawk, when the warrior pursues his enemy, even among many, he only attacks his intended target.

CHAPTER
THREE

He Wore Long Sleeves

I remember sitting beneath an acacia tree,
I can remember sitting beneath an acacia tree
watching the construction of pyramids.

And off in the distance I saw a bald eagle
carrying thirteen arrows and the hope
of a new world order in its talons.

And all around me were signs and symbols
each telling its own story but due to my peripheral
distractions I was unable to decipher their meanings.

So I wrote my interpretations on my arms
in poetic form then concealed then beneath
my long sleeves only to be revealed to
those whom have eyes to see.

See that there's a connection between
the birth rate and the death rate and
the sooner the masses realize this fact
they would have a better understanding
of why we're in Iraq.

Six billion people must be erased from this planet
and the illuminati are doing everything in their
power to accomplish this mission.

So third world nations are systemically targeted
for deletion. And America, oh you Americans if
you can't see that the behaviors that we choose
to engage in are self-destructive then you've

either senile or just plum crazy.

Because for years secret laboratories have been
producing incurable diseases while vegetation
and live stock are contaminated with deadly
bacteria.

But who cares?

You continue pursue your careers
at any cost so if she decides to have
unsafe sex and catches the bug then that's
her loss.

And it shouldn't have to be that way but that's
how it is, complete control of your so called freedoms
is the illuminati's main objective and they will decide
who dies or lives.

So there's a new link in the food chain
and humans are ascending to the top of the list
so survival of the fittest is now upon us.

Stringed Merchants

Sitting on a park bench I stroke the
keys of my notebook as I watch each
disassociated human being walk by
with the look of confusion on their face
as if they were misplaced within this

capitalistic controlled rat race.
Preoccupied with the mundane thoughts
of retirement, life insurance,
and college tuition for their children.

So, I sit back and enjoy the side show
and come to the realization that humans
are no more than puppets on a string
waiting for the puppet master to command
them to do their thing.

The wind blows and the aroma of red roses
is now in the air, then the scene changes
from dogs urinating on trees
into a four car pileup on main street.

The lights went out and the merchants
knew not what to do so they waited, and waited,
and waited and then BANG! Four cars mangled.

Four strangers are now intimate for all the wrong
reasons special ops agents are sleeping with the enemy
while committing espionage and treason.

Xbox, PlayStation, and the internet are the new

educators of our children, 13 year-old girls are
dressing like women and are quick to lie on
their back to please those that appeal them.

And the concern of the stringed merchants
are hollow like comatose patients in the
hospital their response, is null and void.

Until incidents like, passenger loaded bombs
hurling into world trade towers and white
collar criminals serving minimal time and
presidents receiving blow jobs on the job.

With eyes closed wide shut, you only see life
through the master's perspective, subjected to
poverty, unsatisfactory medical conditions
and serving life sentences in prison.

How many shark attacks will it take for you
to realize that you don't belong in the water?
I tend to believe that semtex explosives are
surgically implanted into the cerebral cortex
to keep you in order.

For example, subdivisions are preemptive
concentration camps, just wait until the next
terrorist attack. and you'll see how fast your
freedom of movement will be impeded.

Siege by your own government
and your constitutional rights.

Crooked Dreams

Purple rain drops, blue sunsets
and shattered moonbeams
are the things of crooked dreams.

Luciferian beings disguised as politicians
who tells crooked lies
that leads you to the voting booths
like sheep to the slaughter.

Gum drop silhouettes doing pirouettes
on floors wet,
shot through the heart
crystal clear eyes wept.

Pockets full of anger, hate and discontent
fading in and out of parallel dimensions
stocked with penitentiaries, your soul's for rent.

Planetary alignments meteorite showers
drug dealers moonlights as crooked cops
sell drugs from their patrol cars as they
patrol the block.

Executive order 11-0-5-1, authorizes FEMA
to place you beneath the gun.
Dropping bombs on Iraq and eradicating other
smaller 3rd world countries
but turns a blind eye
to the crime going on in this country.

Conspiracy theory barcodes register everything

That's bought, the NSA, FBI, and CIA
no longer have to tap your phones,
satellites from high up taps right into your very
thoughts. Pandora's box ejecting six headed

demons by the 3's governmental extortion is
unequivocal proof that the slave survivors will
never receive restitution.

Because the powers to be are more concerned
with who has WMD's instead of focusing on
the sanitation practices of the industries
responsible for mad cow disease.

Prison walls hold the atrocities committed by
the hands of two men mentally insane,
one was captured hiding in a spider hole
and the other now controls the game.

Purple rain drops, blue sunsets, and
shattered moonbeams
are the things of crooked dreams.

Jesus Returned to the Ghetto

I had a dream,
I had a dream that Jesus returned to the
ghetto accompanied by two metallic dragons
manufactured by glock, saggin pants
and his hair in locks.

His street rat appearance was received
with curiosity as well as apprehension,
therefore he was treated with extreme prejudice.

So he sat in the center of city hall square
and held conversations with pigeons
because they had no concern with how he looked
just the daily bread he fed them.

And as the multitude walked aimlessly
through the courtyard they paid him no attention
but fear of the unknown held them captive.
So they stood in bewilderment.

Then suddenly Jesus stood and yelled out
from Jacksonville to Israel
death awaits the uninformed
and the streets are colored crimson.

And it doesn't matter if you're young or old
your story will be documented on granite.
But some will be untold,
only maggots will have the intimate details
because you are now sleep like sand.

Traveling at right angles life is mathematics
but the world is off balance so now have
lambs devouring wolves
and parents are afraid of their children.

And street prophets earn profits
by making the congregation empty their pockets.
While elders are working well into their seventies
because they invested their future with the wrong
broker and STDs are distributed like candy, because

brothers don't care where they stick their poker.
Commercial airliners are used as bombs
the French Quarter smells of rotten corpse
and there was a conspiracy in Dallas
that shook the nation.

I taught in the pyramids of Egypt
my secrets lay in the Vatican
Greek philosophers like Plato and Socrates
were nothing but common tomb raiders.

They said I died on the cross for your sins
but your sins continue to shake the heavens
and you refuse to count your blessings.

But yet you patiently wait
for
my
return
it should be obvious that
I'm
already

here.

Look into the eyes of the young black males
right before the cops put that bullet in their chest.
Look into the eyes of the young black females
who are raped before they develop any chest.
That's
where
you
will
find me.

Unwritten

There are no political agendas in the
inner cities therefore there are no troops
or military convoys navigating through
city streets protecting me from the enemy.

Where are those brave journalists who are
willing to sacrifice their lives to tell my story?
Inkless pens scribbles across empty canvases
translation, my story is unwritten.

Because I do not own any oil fields
that supports a porous economy
but the fight for Iraqis freedom is
displayed like the world series on my TV.

While in Jacksonville an eighth grader
is shot to death while reading a book.
And now her parents have to live with
hallow memories.

However in the alleys of Thailand they located
the alleged suspect in a Colorado murder case.
Only to discover there's no DNA to tie him to the case.

With no political clout you have no voice,
and with no political clout you are shut out
of all the decisions that matter.

Where is the domestic tranquility that the
constitution so eloquently speaks about?

I just don't know because living from
pay check to pay check is a living hell
and robbing peter just to pay Paul
is the way most of us are living ya'll.

Hezbollah and Israel are at each other's throat,
while Iran and north Korea wants to deploy
WMD's so, possible sanctions are discussed.

But Sudanese women are raped by ruthless
rebels and no one lifts a finger.
And in the hood gunshots on the block
has everyone on edge and five-0 has
no suspects for the four found dead.

But during election time my hoods vote
is an important commodity, but when the
votes are all cast. The hood instantly becomes
a thing of the past.

And having the wrong name in any American
airport, puts you on the terrorist watch list.
But bin laden is still at large and Afghanistan
opium continues to flood American streets.
I guess catching the 9-11 ring leader is left up
to you and me.

Now getting back to my original point, the
classifieds seems to get more news coverage
than any incident in my on my block.

Maybe if I gave away some trade secrets
or commit espionage, CNN, MSNBC and C-Span

would be camped outside of my garage.

Waiting for the story of the decade, with their
cameras aimed and ready to take that
Pulitzer prize winning picture that will
unwrite my story.

Three Minutes

A life span of 180 seconds
is what was allotted
so during my synoptic presence
I stand naked.

Formless and random thoughts
initiates my existence
however fleeting
tomorrow is not promised.

Born knowing I will lose my life
so, I speak of dreams to you
in hopes to inspire you to live.

Live, live with no deceptions
truth matters more than
you'll ever know.

Sliding doors reveal secrets
hidden in plain view.
Molestation of a child broadcasted
through her silent scars
but no one takes heed.

So the mind becomes a warzone
where suicidal thoughts rule.
And now college campuses
are a haven for the active shooter.

Crimson stained text books
line the hallowed halls.

How many rebirths of 180 seconds
are needed to realign the minds
of the walking dead?

Hovering in mid sentence
creation takes place within
the womb of thought.

Feasting off of your pain
horrifying and shocking stories
are narrated behind a microphone.

With each poem death awaits my arrival
but every three minutes I am reborn
to stand before you.
Kicking and screaming
at the top of my lungs
I fight for you.

Callous hands and bloodshot eyes
are my medals of honor.
POW's held captive eagerly
waits for their freedom.

But I'm at the end of this life span
so I'll see you in three minutes.

I Can't Sleep

It's 4:00 am in the morning and I
haven't slept a wink which is odd
because I never had a problem with
arriving at sleep paralysis.

But here it is 4:00 o'clock in the morning
and I and I just can't sleep because I see
this soldier with one eye open and the
other half close.

Because it's been twelve months since he
last tasted his mother's cooking. And he can't
quite grasp the idea that there's a ten year old
boy dressed in a suicide suit, prepared to take his life.

So, he reluctantly squeezes the trigger of his
m16 and as the ten year old falls to his death
this soldier yearns to be in the arms of his mother
to ease the pain.

It's 4:00 am in the morning and I
haven't slept a wink which is odd
because I never had a problem with
arriving at sleep paralysis.

But here it is 4:00 o'clock in the morning
and I and I just can't sleep because I see
a young mother down on her knees crying
because she lost her son to the streets trying
to be a hard drug dealer.

But what he learned was that the street takes
no prisoners and to survive you must have
a ruthless mentality willing to pull out your
glock and pop, pop, pop at the slightest
show of aggression.

But he's not hard like that because he was
raised with morals and to take another man's
life over something as simple as a debt,
he know he'll regret.

So he hesitated before going for his gun and
now he's laid out in his favorite blue suit.
And his mother just doesn't know what to do.

It's 4:00 am in the morning and I
haven't slept a wink which is odd
because I never had a problem with
arriving at sleep paralysis.

But here it is 4:00 o'clock in the morning
and I and I just can't sleep because I see
this lady of the night who's in desperate need
of her next fix.

So at 4:00 am she's out prowling the streets
willing to take on the lowest bidder.

Three will get you a hand job and five
straight sex for five more and she'll wear
a pearl necklace.

But tonight there are no suitors because

the temperature is in the low 20's.
So she camps out at the nearest crack house
where she falls into an eternal sleep.

I still can't sleep.

Nina's Poem

Last night,
last night I sat down with Nina Simone
and during our conversation
Nina looked me in the eyes
and said Bilaal write me a poem.

Write me a poem that that explains
why the blues resurgence wasn't
successful. And why is it that any art form
that give life to the living is ignored
while any steroid using, law violating

athlete gets all the applause. As if they
discovered the cure for cancer
or received the Nobel Peace Prize
for transforming a quadriplegic
into a world class dancer.

I thought I'll be slick
and come up with some intricate rhetoric
but unlike self-serving politicians
I have a conscious.

So my response was simple.
Any attempt to write that poem
would be an injustice.

Because I'm still trying to out
why the have not's still have not
and why some forty years after the
assassination the dream is still a dream.

Hell, we are morally bankrupt
and the family unit is in foreclosure
mom's working a dead end job
and pop's serving his last leg of a three
to nine.

And my little sister just had her second child
and haven't even graduated from high school yet.
I guess the revolutionary mind set
died when the Noble Drew, Marcus and Malcolm
faded off into the sunset.

And we continue to blame the system
for our trails and tribulations
instead of looking into the mirror
and addressing our own demons.

Like, black on black crime,
missing in action father figures
and illicit drug sales perpetuates the erosion
in the black community.

So, Nina I'm sad to say
that the blues resurgence had no chance for
survival when self-deprecation is worn
like a badge of honor.

And life in the ghetto is reserved
for many more generations to come
because we choose to accept the concept
that I'm gonna get mines when my life here
is done.

Inner City Blues

In the still of the night there
is silence, for a mere moment
close your eyes and listen to
the many cries.

Cries of fear, cries of happiness,
cries of life, and cries of death.
Does anyone ever sleep?

Bright lights confusion is
everywhere survival is a
constant battle thoughts whirling
through my head.

Should I take my life or the next
step into the realm of the unknown?
Deep within this infinite reservoir
there's an answer to this madness.

And know for sure that consequences
dictates your choices positive or negative.
Family is cheated if I off myself
but each day I remain in this chaotic world
I lose more of myself.

Subway trains full of chronicles of unknown
successes and failures, stray dogs seems
to receive more empathy than homeless humans.

So now souls are sold on the internet, PayPal vampires

sucking your life dry. While blue moons and purple
skies are manifested through oxycontin spiked
cappuccinos.

So I sit in mournful solitude at some café contemplating
the subtle messages delivered by the poet
who decided to rewrite my life with her pen.

Because my life expectancy is 25 to life,
and I feel like I'm hooked on phonics
because my words just don't seem
to come out right.

So the doctor has me pumped full of medication
for depression but I'm just a brown skin
gentlemen trying to avoid foreclosure
like the rest of them.

Rush hour traffic seems to work best for me
camped out on the street getting much needed sleep
counting skull fragments instead of sheep.

And I know the universe acknowledges me,
so I will defeat my inner demons
when I put down this gun and pick up my pen
and write.

Hear What I Think

You have to admit that the
negative propaganda being released
by the media have Americans
living in a state of perpetual fear.

And the ironic thing about all this
terror talk, is that it's scripted right
down to the very last noun.

And for years we have been saturated
with words like terror, Al Qaida and Taliban

While organizations like the UN secretly
strategize on the starvation of
3 billion people.

And as long as you continue to focus
on the wrong issues
their plan will continue to
go unnoticed.

And your survival would be like
the roll of the dice snake eyes
means the end of your life
but lucky number seven awards you
another day to get up and fight.

But you Americans love being
somewhat comfortable so you
close your eyes and ears
like turning off the lights in your house

not much effort is needed.

So you continue to go about your business
not realizing that your elimination is
incorporated in their agenda.

So I'm compelled to sit here and
break bread with you to try
to figure out the audacity
of such organizations.

Initiating massive floods throughout
the world in an attempt to wipe out
crops which will introduce millions
to a climate of starvation.

And those of us you are smart enough
to grow our own food will be targeted
like any other drug dealer.

Because life sustaining nutrients have
been classified as poisons so they are
extracting all essential enzymes, minerals,
and vitamins from our food source.

Now that's terrorism

Hidden within their clandestine missions
of war, famine, poison, biological diseases,
and mass executions.

Therefore they create super villains
and get you to believe that our freedom
is in jeopardy.

So you accept their diabolical scheme
not knowing that you
are their main target.

Pen-Thoughts

Soar with the eagle and witness greatness. Walk with the chicken and become soup.

She may be beautiful. However that does not mean she possess beauty.

If there is but one thing I could keep from my childhood. Let it be my imagination.

Who are you? What are you? The answer is not what you find in the mirror.

We often give our opinion on matters we have no knowledge of. Know what is not what you think.

While at battle the warrior does not think of victory, defeat, life or death. He only thinks of completing his mission.

With great determination you will accomplish the impossible.

My ancestors I call on you assist me in removing evil from me.

It is best to make the best out of every generation because you cannot go back to one hundred years or so ago.

Contact Info

Twitter@ BilaalMuhammad9
Facebook: BilaalAMuhammad
LinkedIn: Bilaal Muhammad
MySpace: Bilaal Muhammad
Reverbnation: Bilaal Muhammad

RP Enterprise Publishing
25670 Fairview Ave
Hemet, CA 92544
951-927-8042
www.rpenterpriseca.com

Made in the USA
Charleston, SC
26 April 2014